WHO LIVES HERE?

Wendy Madgwick

Illustrated by John Francis

Flying Frog Publishing

This little nest is in a wheat field. The nest is about the size of a tennis ball. A family of tiny creatures lives inside. The babies learn to climb before they can walk. Which family lives here?

A family of field
mice lives inside
this little nest.

A noise has frightened these little animals. They have run back into their burrows! They live under the ground, where it is safe. They are good at digging and make lots of tunnels. Do you know who has a little white tail and lives in a warren?

Rabbits live
in a warren.
It is made up of lots of
tunnels, called burrows.

This home looks just like a big pile of logs in the river. There are animals living inside. These animals have strong, flat tails to help them move through the water. They have very strong teeth too! Who are they?

They are beavers. Their home is called a lodge. Beavers cut down trees with their teeth to build their home.

These babies live high above the ground. Their home is a nest in a tree. Can you see the babies? Their mouths are wide open. They are hungry. Soon their parents will come back with some tasty food.

Birds live in this nest.
The baby birds like to eat
worms and caterpillars.

This house is a hole in the snow. Brrr! Whoever lives here needs a warm coat. The mother digs the hole. Can you see her footprints in the snow? She shelters here during the winter. Her babies are born inside the den.